NATURE'S CYCLES

A BUTTERFLY'S LIFE CYCLE

A.B. CLAMANT

NorwoodHouse Press

Cataloging-in-Publication Data

Names: Clamant, A.B., 1972-.
Title: A butterfly's life cycle / A.B. Clamant.
Description: Buffalo, NY : Norwood House Press, 2026. | Series: Nature's cycles | Includes glossary and index.
Identifiers: ISBN 9781978575493 (pbk.) | ISBN 9781978575509 (library bound) | ISBN 9781978575516 (ebook)
Subjects: LCSH: Butterflies--Life cycles--Juvenile literature.
Classification: LCC QL544.2 C536 2026 | DDC 595.789--dc23

Published in 2026 by
Norwood House Press
2544 Clinton Street
Buffalo, NY 14224

Designer: Rhea Magaro
Editor: Kim Thompson

Photo credits: Cover, p. 1 NeagoneFo/Shutterstock.com; p. 3 Diane Woodcheke/Shutterstock.com;p. 5 TitleStock/Shutterstock.com; p. 6,7 Nikhil Guhagarkar/Shutterstock.com; p. 8 Shuaib_Shot/Shutterstock.com; p. 9 Cathy Keifer/Shutterstock.com; p. 10 dossyl/Shutterstock.com; p. 11 Tom Korcak/Shutterstock.com; p. 13 sangpemotret/Shutterstock.com; p. 14 HamimThohari/Shutterstock.com; pp. 16, 17 Lena Robinson/Shutterstock.com; p. 18 I Wayan Sumatika/Shutterstock.com; p. 21 smutan/Shutterstock.com

Printed in the United States of America

CPSIA compliance information: Batch #CSNHP26: For further information contact Norwood House Press at 1-800-237-9932.

TABLE OF CONTENTS

Where Do Butterflies Come From?

A butterfly flits by on beautiful wings. A caterpillar creeps on branches. The two things have nothing to do with each other, right? Wrong! They are both part of the amazing life **cycle** of butterflies.

Sticky Eggs

All butterflies begin as tiny eggs. Butterflies can lay hundreds of eggs per day.

A male butterfly **fertilizes** eggs while they are still inside the female's body. Then, the female lays the eggs on a plant. She **secretes** a sticky substance like glue that holds the eggs in place.

Hungry Caterpillars

After a week or two, each tiny egg will **hatch**. A butterfly **larva**, also known as a caterpillar, comes out.

Caterpillars are born hungry! They eat their eggshells. They eat the leaves on the plant where they hatched. Then, they eat more leaves.

As a caterpillar eats, its body expands. Its skin gets tight. Then, the skin splits to reveal new skin. This process of shedding skin is called **molting**.

A caterpillar can grow up to 1,000 times its birth weight. It keeps molting as it grows.

After a few weeks, caterpillars stop eating. They find a safe place. They attach to a leaf or a branch and hang upside down. All that eating has given them lots of energy for what comes next.

Big Changes

The caterpillar molts one last time. This time, the skin splits to reveal a shiny outer shell. The insect is now a **chrysalis**. The butterfly is in the **pupa** stage.

Inside the chrysalis, the insect goes through a huge change. Its body breaks down to form something completely new. This change in form is called a **metamorphosis**.

Over seven to ten days, new body parts develop. Four wings, new legs, eyes, and a mouth form.

A Butterfly Is Born!

When the adult butterfly is ready, it breaks free from the chrysalis. It stretches and dries its new wings. Then, it flies!

The Cycle Continues

Many adult butterflies live for only one or two weeks. They are ready to **mate**. It is time to lay eggs and begin the cycle again.

Glossary

chrysalis (KRIS-uh-lis): a butterfly in a quiet stage of development between a caterpillar and an adult; the hard outer shell in which a caterpillar changes into a butterfly

cycle (SYE-kuhl): a series of events that repeat over and over in the same order

fertilizes (FUR-tuh-lize-is): provides the male parts that make a female's eggs able to grow into new life; joins male and female parts during mating

hatch (hach): to break out of an egg to be born

larva (LAHR-vuh): an animal at an early stage of development when it looks completely different from its parents

mate (mate): the pairing of a male and female to produce babies